Before & After

Keishaura West

Before & After

Before & After

Keishaura West

Before & After

Keishaura West

Before & After
Copyright© 2018
Keishaura West

Printed in the United States of America

ISBN: 978-0-692-09885-1

Library of Congress – Catalogued in Publication Data

All rights reserved. No part of this book may be reproduced, stored in a retrieval system, or transmitted in any form or by any means, electronic, mechanical photocopying, recording, or otherwise, without written consent of the publisher except in the case of brief quotations in critical articles or reviews.

First published by dpRochelle 3/12/18

dp*Rochelle*
PO Box 9523
Hampton, Virginia 23670
1(757) 825-0030 | DrIrisPerkins.org

Before & After

DEDICATION

To Mr. Gray:

A salt and peppered hair consistent friend, who has supported my dreams during near death experiences, yet encouraged me to restore harmony within to fulfill a life of vitality, excitement and ultimately success.

Before & After

TABLE OF CONTENTS

---

13   Chapter 1: THE BIRTH OF HER

25   Chapter 2: METAMORPHOSIS

43   Chapter 3: BEYOND THE SURFACE

63   Chapter 4: WE ALL NEED SOMEONE

73   Chapter 5: DON'T GET OUT OF CHARACTER

85   Chapter 6: YOU CAN'T ALWAYS GET WHAT YOU WANT

Before & After

Chapter 1

The Birth of 'Her'

Before & After

Growing up in South Memphis, Tennessee presented peculiar circumstances. I recall living inside of a two-bedroom apartment in which my siblings and I shared space. The apartment complex was small, enclosed and limited; yet, even as a child I knew the outdoor world was my canvass. Walks to school were long and often terrifying. Despite being tall, I was not exempt from bullying.

Most would consider South Memphis as the projects. My mother never allowed us to be viewed as 'project children.' We were well-groomed, well-mannered and at a state of comfort during our childhood. It is safe to say, my siblings and I were hardly faced with difficulties or opposition. We did not reside in that atmosphere long and later moved to East Memphis. As I grew from a child to a teenager, I began experimenting. I never knew where I was headed; however, I knew that I was on a road to fulfillment.

Fast forwarding to the year of 2008, I graduated high school. Most, if not all of my friends were leaving Memphis to attend out of state colleges. I, too, attended college but stayed local. My life had officially become routine. School and work was all I knew, until I met a lawyer one day while working. He was narcissistic and aggressive in his approach. During my shift as a cashier, he asked me, "So are you going to give me your number? I have somewhere to be." "Sigh" . . . I did just as he stated; I gave him my number.

Tyler, the lawyer, and I dated for a few years. I looked to him as a mentor for motivation and aspiration. He was much older than I was, but to be honest, his maturity growth and development were what intrigued me. At approximately twenty years of age, I sat on the couch, leaning against Tyler, rambling on while crying my eyes out, and stating how I was not successful enough. Tyler responded calmly, "You are only twenty. Relax. You have time." I shook my head in disagreement.

Let's pause for a second. Tyler used my age as a form of complacency, and there are people who share a similar outlook. If you are a person with a vision of burning desire, shoot for it! Do not allow your age (despite how old or young you are) to depict a level of accomplishment. Okay. Let's resume!

After engaging in conversation with Tyler, I secretly pondered about joining the military. I oftentimes drifted into an oasis when Tyler went to sleep. Our relationship was rocky and was nothing short of abusive; Tyler was jealous with stalker tendencies and I would not leave because he took care of me. By this time, I was no longer working and was very much so an unofficial housewife.

I recall being at a local store not far from where we resided. Unknowingly, Tyler saw me interacting with a local police officer. I had no idea he was near! After walking into our home, he demanded I remove my underwear so that he could smell them. He wanted to know if I had been sexually involved with the police officer with whom I interacted. Bizarre, I know! I refused and he pushed me onto the sofa, raised his fist and punched me above my right eyebrow (a scar which I still have to this day). Blood immediately rolled down my face. I shouted, kicked, cried, but one thing I did not do was LEAVE. Anger and resentment fermented within; yet, I could not leave. This man had a hold on me—partially because I allowed it. In my mind, I owed him. I was so young and figured because he was my provider, it was morally right for me to stay with him as a form of loyalty. When he and I argued, I would shout that I was going to leave once I joined the military. At the time, that was the only way I could truly escape 'Tyler's hold.'

Before & After

Chapter 2

METAMORPHOSIS

Before & After

Boy was life filled with many roller coasters after joining the military. Joining the military was a shift in pace like no other. I underwent several transitional phases and am currently undergoing more. Walking into MEPS (Military Entrance Processing Station) was the beginning of my personal evolution. There were civilians everywhere asking for social security numbers, taking photos of you and obtaining as much personal information one could imagine. I recall a tall, stocky, and mature in age male asking about my love life. At the time I did not quite understand what he was getting at. Especially since I was trying to escape an abusive relationship. To say the least, he warned me of the many males I was sure to encounter.

He stated, "Your hardest decision will be choosing which man to date."

I did not know what that meant but accepted it as truth and prepared for basic training. *I can say, being a female in the military the least of your worries are male attention. LOL. We get first draft pick sort of speak!*

My loved ones watched me depart to Memphis International Airport, only later to arrive at O'Hare International Airport. At this point I can say, the 'True Evolution of Ms. West' commenced. As I entered into a state of uncertainty the continuous question of, 'Are you tired of living life with limitation?" probed my mind daily. Yet, this thought was not sparked coincidentally because I had asked, prayed, and meditated for it. I had always told myself that I was destined for greatness.

After basic training, I was quickly sent overseas to Sasebo, Japan. Living in another country, being without family and adapting to a different set of traditions and customs were shockers to me. *"I am from Memphis was my thought! WTF is this?!"* I was not use to people driving on the opposite side of the road, fully dressed in long sleeves and pants during the summer, extremely narrow two-lane roads, people bowing in cherry blossom Kimonos, and wearing freaking surgical masks. All I did was cry and relied heavily on majestic strength to get me through. After the tears ran out, there was nothing more left to do but take this "new" challenge and turn it into a positive.

At the time, embracing what was around me meant walking into the unknown. I knew it had to be done, and quite frankly, I had minimal choice but to breakthrough. Eventually the unfamiliar became familiar. As one adapts to their surroundings, there are but two things you can do—overcome or lose. One thing I quickly learned was to never allow my current position in life to consume me, especially since I was not where I desired to be.

I began meeting people as I gained exposure by being super cool and maintaining a fashionable style. Let me tell you, being 5'11 in a country where the average female height is 5'2 presented trend difficulties. However, I made it work! I paid extra detail to my attire, physique and hair. My extensions were sleek, straight and approximately 22 inches. I also learned to sew my extensions and 'beat my face' with MAC cosmetics. Work, gym, and partying were all I knew. I drove boats for a living at this time. Our eight-hour shifts were easy breezy, and half of it was spent at the gym. In the military, one must be a chameleon who is able to juggle multiple things at once. Was partying a bad thing? Absolutely not. However, too much of anything has the potential of being bad. I was not taking school seriously, nor was I maximizing the overseas experience. The partying blossomed into something short of a problem. Remember, I always destine myself for greatness, but I was cognizant enough to know this process was sure to take time.

We all know the stereotype associated with sailors. It's safe to say it is true. We can drink anyone under a table...and potentially to death. The frequent consumption of alcohol increased my tolerance. While drinking, I would turn into someone else, someone that people grew to hate. I found myself apologizing prior to an alcohol intake and again, the day after; my unknown problem was offensive.

Most overseas bases have base clubs with alcohol which took full control of my actions. As people approached me, I would immediately turn away, act snobbish, or reluctantly greet them if they did not fit into what I thought was acceptable during that time. Base clubs had a platform that was elevated from the dance floor. I would assume my throne at this particular area because it separated my friends and I from the masses. We were 'higher' than others in essence. This behavior was hurtful, obnoxious and embarrassed people. I was told by my friends and strangers that I was viewed as a horrible person and deep down inside, I knew it. Despite being beautiful, arrogance took over me. I quickly learned 'beauty' meant nothing if the interior was dark, shallow, and cold!

Reality set in when friends grew distant then eventually

vanished. There were countless nights of tears and remorse. There are only so many apologies a person can accept. I took full responsibility of my wrong which led to a deep depression. Things were dreary and cloudy. While being alone I was falling downward and came short of rock bottom. I conjured enough strength to seek help, yet man was not the answer. What I was after could only be obtained from a majestic spirit. This force of superior being could be granted but would not come overnight. This process was a wakeup call and a very critical step to entering the next phase.

One beauty of life reveals no obstacle is infinite. Patience and timing has a way of smoothing itself out. With that being said, things got better for me. In order to maintain integrity, I would be dishonest if I posed the story of being tribulation free; in fact, that is far from the truth. Realistically, obstacles are presenting themselves this very day. Setbacks vary in situations. Some may witness minor setbacks, while others undergo critical ones, but I will inform you that everyone has their fair share. As I mature, the totality of real things and events occur. Trials are in place to assist with the unexpected interruption of negative habits. When I fail, or react out of habit, I realize afterwards what could have been done differently. Once flaws reveal themselves, civilized individuals immediately work towards correcting those actions. Maintaining a sense of self-awareness is paramount. Knowing 'you' disables the enemy. The enemy is unable to destroy you if he or she has no ammunition. As changes begin to occur it will cause a ripple effect of discomfort. You must anticipate and continue progressing until your flaws evolve, and then revamp.

Chapter 3

Beyond the Surface

Before & After

Keishaura West

Being in the military is a great stepping stone for those deciding to take a leap of uncertainty. This enables those who are willing to fight for our country while developing a sense of substance. As African American young ladies, we enter with preconceived notions or 'branded' stereotypes. This in itself causes unnecessary stress. I noticed that every action, gesture, and statement went into scrutiny during interactions with those of a different ethnicity. Being viewed as an angry Black woman is universal in America, but widely believed in the military. Most make fun of it as the military is not as bad as people believe. Yet this notion brings about mental fatigue. While others have the luxury of focusing primarily on their goals, we as females and those females who are African Americans have to work double time, or twice as hard, to execute goals. At times I lost motivation. My efforts were being underappreciated—at least I thought. I was more focused on behavior and of body language than my actual job. It became challenging. I wanted to quit, yet that whisper stated to keep pressing forward. There were times the stigma of being an angry Black woman presented itself.

    I know I know that I just discussed preconceived notions and admitted to proving that stereotype to be true, but GEESH sometimes you get tired! Everyone has their day. I do not condone losing yourself in the midst of pressure, but it is guaranteed to happen. Suddenly, a light bulb switched on. A mental fight will win a physical fight every time. With each day, one should be wiser, mentally stronger, and physically better than the day before. If you are aware, in this case stereotypes of Black females, work towards being the change, work towards disassociating yourself with any negative stigma. A preconceived notion does not stop with attitudes. In fact, it does not matter your race, gender, or religion, do your best to counteract it.

After entering this state of knowing, I proceeded toward a

different path. This is why maintaining a keen hold on one's personality and individuality is detrimental. Life has shown me that when a person knows what bothers you most, they will forever be able to control you. Are you one to maintain control of your life or give it away to anyone witty enough to take possession? I have learned that people will only do what you allow. If you wish to be a walking doormat, then expect second or third-class treatment. However, if you view yourself in the utter most royalty, then guess what? So, will others. Remain humble but love thy self-first.

Upon loving yourself be mindful that you are subject to being judged. I mean, realistically we do it all the time. The only difference is that some people are weakened by it while others are empowered. Should this be an acceptable action of natural occurrence? What is normal? Why are we as humans quick to shun or disown someone that does not fit into the conforming type? I am sure to not be the only person experiencing this - am I? Have you ever entered a space and demanded attention without saying a word? This feeling of self-assurance and confidence can be intimidating. It appears to not matter if your demeanor is welcoming. The feeling of self-validation for others is not their prototype. So often than not, I have been asked the questions: *Why do you walk that way? Why must you uphold a pristine posture? Why do you feel so entitled? Do you think you are better than us?* It took some time to understand why I was greeted with similar questions. The inquiry of others caused me to think something was wrong. I continuously questioned who I was as a person. After all of my soul searching and constant efforts to be better—daily, weekly, monthly and annually—I still allowed people to detect and trump my weakness. I found myself working towards pleasing others.

There were moments I lowered myself to elevate others. Upon encountering new people, I caught myself explaining who I am and the reason for maneuvering the way I did. When I say, 'every encounter' - literally! It was horrible! Some people would listen, and others would smile and nod in total confusion. I looked like a crazy person meeting people while giving unwanted explanations.

Out of all conversation topics, I chose an unwanted request as the opening statement. Can you imagine how draining, discomforting and self-detaching this action was? Heck, over time I rolled with the punches. I had no control of anyone's perception of me. As long as I had an inviting demeanor, their thoughts had nothing to do with me, but were an internal reflection of themselves. After all, society will always find a flaw in your being. People will go out their way to correct your deficiencies while theirs need so much assembly that 'Iyana' could not fix their life. Then this idea sparked within me…maybe I am not built to blend in. Maybe I am destined to be the leading force to aid others in maximizing their potential. I have always been open to change. Change is good as long as it leads to a better you. However, to become different for the sole purpose of pleasing others is never a good disposition.

We as humans are made to follow the natural flow of life's directions. Interrupting life's natural flow can bring unwanted transformations that could have been deflected if you were not resistant. Reflect on those moments in life when you were given 'warning' signals but proceeded anyhow. Somehow you failed to heed the warnings. It was not until life took its course and you had no choice but to consider the actions of yours that took place. In that moment of solitude, you think, "If only I had taken heed to those warnings." The same rule applies from an internal point. In other words, embrace you! Only you and a select few know your journey. Remain humble, but never apologize for having the quality of being certain.

I recall exiting the library in middle school. The librarian stopped me as I bypassed her and stated, "Keishaura, fix your posture. Never walk with your shoulders slumped forward.

Learn to elongate your frame." From that moment forward, I maintained a keen eye on the position or bearing of my body.

Working to improve you in every aspect should be a continuous act. I will never grow complacent; you should not either! If you are relaxed and nonchalant on most things, this is the ONE thing with which you should not be apathetic. Once you become aware of this evolution, it provides you with an intuitive response. As you, like me, blossom into greatness, there will be moments of discomfort. Discomfort bestowed upon you, from others will enable you to detect their energy. While traveling to your destination some people will remain the same while others will voluntarily or involuntarily are forced to retreat. I was not expecting this to occur, but peace and stillness helped prepare for its occurrence. Different stages in life will cause a continuous cycle of entrance and exiting. This process forces us into the state of uneasiness. There are only so much we are willing to accept prior to putting our foot down and fighting back. We as humans, or any living mammal, do not like physical or mental discomfort. You begin to strategize ways to remove the 'parasite'. With each second you fathom strength to combat. Those seconds turn into minutes, those minutes into hours and those hours into days and so on and so forth. As you continue to strive to overcome, at the end you realize you were not defeated. Continue to improve by identifying and differentiating those threatened by your evolution and those willing to assist with the next stage in life.

Chapter 4

We All Need Someone

Before & After

Keishaura West

Where did I get off thinking I could survive in life alone? As a young adult, believe it or not, this was the extent of my mental capacity. Consumed with pride, arrogance and, conceit - I was too foolish to realize I was on the path of self-destruction. I had this narcissistic thinking that things were going to be my way or no way! "Non-negotiable" was an ideology of mine. Boy was I in for a rude awakening!

A surprised and unpleasant discovery that was mistaken was sure to follow. I recall commuting from Japan to the United States due to a beloved one battling an illness. After approximately three months of going back and forward, I received that forbidden call that a loved one had passed. My entire world came trickling down. Initially I cried. The next step was to make preparations to physically see a 'lovely lady' for the final time. Late nights and early moments brought about deep thoughts. Who could I call to vent, cry to or simply from whom will I receive comfort? I had no one! Yes, I relied heavily on spiritual Father, but there are times we prefer a physical being. Having a person there to rub my back, wipe the tears away, and allow me to release all of the built-up emotions was something I strongly desired. Experiencing loneliness during a time of need opened my eyes.

There were people saying basic things like: *"Are you ok? Call me if you need anything."* But to me those are common core gestures people state during moments of grief. In layman's terms, it was the right thing to do! My friends were nonexistent, due to the negative actions of an intoxicated me. Who wants to be an acquaintance to a person that intentionally humiliates, and make others feel less than worthy simply because they were not aesthetically fortunate? To tell someone or a group of people they could not 'sit with us' or they were not 'welcomed by us' (us meaning my then - friends) were actions of a person who was sure to be knocked off their 'high-horse.' When genuine support came, I felt horrible. Months before, I was too self-consumed to say something so simple as 'Hi' or participate in functions when invited, yet the same individuals went above and beyond to assist with my internal healing.

How do you fully show your appreciation? How do you fathom such superb acts of kindness after showing the opposite? My actions displayed appreciation and thankfulness, but to me, that was not enough. Experiencing the burial of my mother brought a great deal of humility. This became a turning point in my life. Tranquility graced me as happy memorable moments trampled the mind. Life revealed to me that you never know who you need until you are in need.

In that moment, I made a mandated as a personal obligation to serve others. In fact, I have discovered the tithes you give for being on earth is to be of good service to others. Actions as such are not always accompanied with bad situations. Events, homeless shelters, research facilities or anything involving those of greater or less fortunate...I assist! One thing life has shown is when people are in need, they enter a vulnerable state—the humbling, rewarding, and valuable lesson of being in service to others enables you to see the bigger picture. Everything is not about you! Sense expanding my horizon to this basic concept of human existence, I have freely entered Nirvana.

Chapter 5

Don't Get Out of Character

Before & After

People, stop allowing others to get you out of character! Point blank! Period! Many times people see a light shining from within you that has yet to seep through! People will pull and push until everything has shifted and the blame is now on you! Those who see no wrong in their actions somehow become a victim which should not hold any substance in your life.

    There was a point in my life where I would allow others to push me to the limit. At the time, if only I vociferously informed others of how I truly felt about them they would back off. Unfortunately, my actions did the opposite. Pointing my index finger, choosing colorful language to emphasize my perspective about a person or situation only made me a silent laughing stock. People knew which buttons to press. People knew my weaknesses. Being quick tempered enabled others to spark a negative reaction. After a while being snappy and having a knee-jerk response grew old. There are things in our personal process from that we cannot return. I began to rationalize every situation - from start to finish. Now, I view myself as a realist. As I write this book, it is important for me to remain authentic in hopes of preventing others who are/have similar life experiences. When evaluating a picture, it is paramount to view interest of the two.

As I have previously mentioned pride and arrogance is the quickest way to fail therefore in despite of the pedestal I once rode, I have never had issues with apologizing. After stating your peace assesses, reassess, assess more until you reach a consensus. The consensus should aide in determining to where that person stands in your life. Remember, you are responsible for your happiness. Those who blatantly take it for granted should not be of any value as you transcend. I have learned that it takes more energy to exert negative thoughts and actions versus doing the opposite. As you progress in life there comes the blossoming moment of being tuned in to self. When it occurs, you are able to realize your purpose in life while remaining firm in your beliefs, value and effort. During this royal journey people from all avenues will begin to attack you - brace yourself for shock! It will sting and bite like no pain you have ever felt before. The people inflicting this pain are not limited to strangers or co-workers. Individuals causing harm are being received from brother, sister, close relatives and even those with whom you share a child. While remaining calm and shining like the beautiful lotus you are, minimize details you share during interaction with those members accordingly. The funny thing is that it all trickles down to people fearing that you may surpass them. Granted, nobody knows the trouble you have seen.

Everyone experiences tribulations, yet people can be one-dimensional when wanting someone to remain stagnant. Truth be told there is room at the top; the bottom is over-crowded! All in all, identify and assess each situation prior to reacting. Determine from what source the unwanted notion is coming from. If it is being released from a person who does not hold a fixed billet in your life, remove yourself. Do not grant pleasure to someone who does not stand precedent in your life to quickly interrupt it. Why should Negative Nancy or Frowning Fred be given satisfaction? I am still practicing what

I preach, but with practice comes perfection.

Before & After

Chapter 6

You Can't Always Get What You Want...

Before & After

Keishaura West

I have stood through adversity in a way that allows me to reflect and smile. During tragic times, I wondered if it would ever end. Well, my friend, I am sure to tell you it does! As I ponder, I realize difficult misfortunes are a part of the circle of life. You must endure some sort of pain if you aspire to 'Be Somebody.' Remember, I always destined myself for greatness, as you should too! I knew there was a purpose to be fulfilled, and that while fulfilling it, I discovered life was not solely about me. This determination enabled me to showcase the 'After.'

I am feminine, resilient, optimistic and encouraging. I float through life like an oasis providing refuge and relief. When I wake in the morning, I give praise to the highest up. Upon getting my day started, I input a smile. I mean, smiles are contagious and even more infectious when they are pearly white! *Wink Wink*

I have been humbled as humility is my greatest attribute. I have a stance to rebuild anyone that crosses paths for the better. I take pride in having an open and welcoming demeanor. I walk with confidence and grace. My stride mimics Naomi Campbell in her prime.

When the body and mind align, you become of substance. In fact, I feel better than I did in my early twenties. Granted, I am an active gym member while self-presentation is especially significant.

Become a person with an action in course of execution.

'The After' showcases a relaxed outlook towards things that are beyond control. I have learned to reserve my energy for things that 'matter'. Remember, we discussed earlier the importance of prioritizing people and situations? Yes, we are tying it all in now. I have developed inner strength. I have learned to keep my dreams to myself while relying solely on spiritual guidance. I believe people that are meant to be a part of your journey will surface. You shall never have to force anyone's support. As for my 'After, 'life has revealed a sense of outcomes that continue to aide in an ongoing transformation. Who am I? This question continues to resonant.

    I am Her.
    I am She.
    I am We!
    Sheesh, isn't life good?

Keishaura West

More Copies Available on

www.Amazon.com

Before & After

Keishaura West

Before & After

www.ingramcontent.com/pod-product-compliance
Lightning Source LLC
Chambersburg PA
CBHW072101290426
44110CB00014B/1777